Flashrevise
Pocketbook

A2 US Government & Politics

Philip Allan Updates, an imprint of Hodder Education, an Hachette UK company, Market Place, Deddington, Oxfordshire OX15 0SE

Orders

Bookpoint Ltd, 130 Milton Park, Abingdon, Oxfordshire OX14 4SB
tel: 01235 827827   fax: 01235 400401   e-mail: education@bookpoint.co.uk

Lines are open 9.00 a.m.–5.00 p.m., Monday to Saturday, with a 24-hour message answering service. You can also order through our website: www.philipallan.co.uk

First published in 2005 as *Flashrevise Cards*

Impression number   5   4   3   2   1
Year   2014   2013   2012   2011   2010

Printed in Spain

Hachette UK's policy is to use papers that are natural, renewable and recyclable products and made from wood grown in sustainable forests. The logging and manufacturing processes are expected to conform to the environmental regulations of the country of origin.

P01796

From independence to union

Q1 What were the Articles of Confederation?

Q2 What kind of government did they create?

Q3 Why did the various states decide to try to frame a new Constitution in 1787?

Q4 Who were the Founding Fathers?

ANSWERS ▶▶

Treaty of Paris (1783) secured independence; Philadelphia Convention (1787) framed a new constitution

A1 In 1781, the states agreed to enter into a loose *confederacy* as opposed to a truly *federal* or a *unitary* system.

A2 There was no national executive (such as a president) nor any national judiciary. There was a Congress consisting of representatives from each state but this 'central government' only had power over limited areas, e.g. foreign policy, relations with Native Americans and coinage.

A3 Writers such as Alexander Hamilton were expressing the view that the Articles had created a system that was too *decentralised*.

A4 They were the 55 representatives of the various states who met at Philadelphia in 1787 to frame a new constitutional settlement.

***examiner's* note** This card is background information, which is unlikely to form the basis of an examination question in itself.

1 ANSWERS

Socioeconomic profile

Q1 John F. Kennedy described the USA as 'a nation of immigrants'. What did he mean?

Q2 How ethnically diverse is the US population today?

Q3 In what ways does the sheer scale and diversity of the USA impact on its political life?

ANSWERS

A1 The USA was founded upon successive waves of immigration. Between 1820 and 1914 around 30 million immigrants arrived. Kennedy was, therefore, referring to the fact that virtually all modern US citizens can trace their ancestry back to immigrant families.

A2 In 2009 around 75% of the US population was white (excluding 30 million white Hispanics). Black Americans made up 12.4%, and around 15.4% (either black or white) were Hispanic.

A3 The USA covers six time zones and has the widest possible diversity in population, geography and climate. A lot of political power is held at state rather than federal government level. National parties keep their platforms vague in order to retain the broadest appeal.

***examiner's* note** Use this information in conjunction with material on voting behaviour (see Card 70).

ANSWERS

Political culture

Q1 Is it possible to identify the key elements that characterise US political culture?

Q2 What is the 'American Dream'?

Q3 Has US political culture changed significantly in recent years?

ANSWERS

the attitudes, values and beliefs that shape political behaviour within a country

A1 A belief in liberty, limited government, laissez-faire economics, individualism and the 'American Dream' could all be seen as key elements.

A2 This is the notion that any US citizen can succeed as long as he or she is prepared to work hard and make sacrifices.

A3 Individuals are said to be increasingly isolated and unlikely to participate in political activity — the 'Bowling Alone' phenomenon identified by Robert Putnam. Society is also said to be increasingly 'Balkanised', with different ethnic groups living and working within their own communities rather than being assimilated.

***examiner's* note** Although answer 3 paints a rather negative view, some more encouraging signals came out of the USA in the wake of 9/11 (see Card 4) and in the improved turnout at the 2008 Presidential Election.

 ANSWERS

The USA post-9/11

Q1 Give an example of the way in which 9/11 affected US political culture.

Q2 How did the events of September 2001 affect the relationship between the three branches of the federal government?

Q3 Give an example of the way in which 9/11 led to a change in the relationship between the federal government and state governments.

ANSWERS

the unprecedented events of 11 September 2001 led to a number of changes in US society and politics

A1 A Gallup poll in October 2001 found that 13% of US citizens felt they could trust the government in Washington 'just about always' — up from 4% in 2000.

A2 Post-9/11 George W. Bush found it relatively easy to get measures through Congress. The Democrats appeared unwilling to criticise the president publicly while the country was 'under attack'. The Supreme Court was similarly passive.

A3 It led to the creation of a new federal department — the Office of Homeland Security — which took ultimate control of anti-terrorist measures away from individual states.

***examiner's* note** Similarly, dramatic changes in relationships and attitudes took place during the Vietnam War and after Watergate. Most, however, faded with time.

 ANSWERS

Intentions of the Founding Fathers

Q1 Why is it difficult to identify the intentions of the Founding Fathers?

Q2 Identify the position taken by one or more of the Founding Fathers during the negotiations at Philadelphia.

Q3 How much value is there in trying to identify the intentions of the Founding Fathers as we endeavour to isolate the meaning of the Constitution and apply it to each new age?

ANSWERS

the embodiment of the political aims of the Founding Fathers (the 'spirit' of the Constitution)

A1 There were 55 delegates at Philadelphia and, as Alistair Cooke noted, the final settlement was based on three key principles, 'compromise, compromise and compromise'.

A2 Alexander Hamilton believed in a strong federal government but feared that pure democracy might lead to mob rule. Thomas Jefferson advocated the separation of powers and limited government. James Madison favoured an entrenched bill of rights.

A3 Some believe that those interpreting the document should look more to the demands of the twenty-first century than to the 'original intent' of those who wrote it in 1787.

examiner's note Some Supreme Court judges believe that the constitution should be applied literally. They are known as *strict constructionists* (see Card 44).

(5) **ANSWERS**

Framing the Constitution

Q1 Which concerns were common to all of those who met at Philadelphia?

Q2 Identify one way in which the needs of the smaller and larger states were balanced?

Q3 How did the Founding Fathers balance their desire to avoid tyranny with their fear of pure democracy?

ANSWERS

the process of negotiating and arriving at a new constitutional settlement

A1 The Founding Fathers wanted to create a more meaningful central government, while guaranteeing state and individual rights. They wanted to avoid a return to the 'tyranny of British rule'.

A2 The Connecticut Compromise, proposed by Connecticut delegate Roger Sherman, offered a solution. Seats in the House would be apportioned in relation to a state's population, while the Senate would have two representatives from each state, regardless of population.

A3 Mechanisms such as the Electoral College (see Card 60) were established to combat the fear that democracy, unchecked, could become 'mobocracy' — the rule of the uneducated, politically ignorant mob.

***examiner's* note** The Founding Fathers did *not* regard what they created at Philadelphia as being a 'model Constitution'.

 ANSWERS

Separation of powers

Q1 What roles did Baron Montesquieu feel should be performed by the three branches of government?

Q2 Why were overlapping or fused powers seen as a potential cause of tyranny?

Q3 How complete was the separation of powers adopted in the US Constitution?

ANSWERS ▶▶

in the USA, the three main branches of government — executive, legislature and judiciary — are separate

A1 The legislature was to make laws; the executive branch was to put these laws into effect; the judiciary was to interpret and adjudicate disputes arising from the law.

A2 Montesquieu felt that tyranny could result if the powers to make, execute and enforce the laws were held by a single branch, or if key individuals were members of two or more branches at the same time.

A3 The Founding Fathers saw that a total separation of powers could result in permanent gridlock. Instead, they put in place a modified system of shared powers accompanied by checks and balances. Richard Neustadt referred to this as 'separated institutions, sharing powers'.

***examiner's* note** Montesquieu saw the British system of government as one to be admired, despite its fusion of executive and legislative.

 **7** **ANSWERS**

Checks and balances

Q1 Why did the Founding Fathers build checks and balances into the US system of government?

Q2 Outline some of the key controls that operate on the three branches of the federal government.

Q3 In practice, how effective are the checks and balances in preventing one branch from dominating or obstructing the other two?

ANSWERS

A1 Checks and balances provide enough linkage for the government to work but bar any one branch from dominating.

A2 The president can veto bills passed but Congress can override the veto with a $\frac{2}{3}$ majority in each chamber. The president's foreign policy powers are similarly limited by Congress and the president's appointments require Senate confirmation. The Supreme Court can void presidential and congressional actions if it judges them unconstitutional.

A3 Checks and balances are often less effective in practice than they look on paper. The Supreme Court has no means of enforcing its judgements and so is reliant upon the president and/or Congress.

***examiner's* note** In emergencies (e.g. post-9/11), Congress often relaxes its checks to allow the president greater freedom.

 ANSWERS

Federalism in the USA

Q1 What is the significance of the 10th Amendment?

Q2 In practice, how rigid is the divide between federal and state authority?

Q3 How has US federalism developed since the ratification of the Constitution?

ANSWERS

a system in which political power is shared between federal and state governments

A1 The 10th Amendment establishes the notion of 'reserved powers', under which individual states retain full control over certain areas.

A2 In times of national crisis (e.g. post-9/11), states often cede power to the federal government so it can coordinate efforts nationally.

A3 Under dual federalism (1780s–1920s), the federal and various state governments each had separate spheres of authority. Following the Wall Street Crash, cooperative federalism (1930s–60s) saw the federal government become more involved in coordinating policy efforts nationally. The 'New Federalism' of presidents such as Nixon and Reagan sought to return power to the states.

***examiner's* note** The change in the size, status and world role of the USA since 1787 has necessitated some growth in federal government power.

 **9** **ANSWERS**

Amending the Constitution

Q1 How can the Constitution be amended?

Q2 Why has it proven so hard to amend the US Constitution formally?

Q3 Give an example of how difficult the constitutional amendment process can be.

ANSWERS

the process of altering the US Constitution by formal amendment of the document

A1 The formal amendment process is in two stages. The proposal must be backed by a $\frac{2}{3}$ majority in both houses or by conventions in at least $\frac{2}{3}$ of the states (never used). Ratification requires the support of $\frac{3}{4}$ (currently 38) of the states.

A2 The 'supermajorities' required for proposal and ratification are difficult to achieve.

A3 The proposed Equal Rights Amendment passed the proposal stage in Congress in 1972 but was ratified by only 35 of the 38 states required, even though the deadline was put back to 1982.

***examiner's* note** The ability of the Supreme Court to reinterpret the Constitution over time through judicial review allows the document to evolve and remain relevant. Regular Acts of Congress and conventions also add to the constitutional framework.

The Bill of Rights

Q1 Outline the range of activities that the 1st Amendment has come to protect.

Q2 Explain what is meant by the terms '1st Amendment absolutism' and '1st Amendment balancing'.

Q3 Summarise the other key rights protected by the Bill of Rights.

ANSWERS

A1 These range from the right of Amish children not to attend public schools beyond the 8th grade (the 'free exercise' clause) to the right of women to strip (the 'freedom of speech and the press' clause).

A2 1st Amendment absolutism is the belief that the 1st Amendment guarantees should be taken literally. 1st Amendment balancing holds that these guarantees be balanced against the needs of others as provided for elsewhere in the constitution.

A3 The 2nd Amendment entrenches the 'right to bear arms'; Amendments IV to VIII concern the rights of the accused; the 10th Amendment protects state rights.

***examiner's* note** The constitutional protection of rights does not stop with the Bill of Rights. Other amendments have also been important (see Card 12).

(11) ANSWERS

Other constitutional amendments

Q1 What kinds of areas have been addressed by the 17 constitutional amendments ratified since 1791?

Q2 In what ways do these amendments add to the protection of individual liberties enshrined in the Bill of Rights?

Q3 Identify areas in which further constitutional amendments have been mooted.

ANSWERS ▶▶

A1 Seven relate to elections. The 15th and 19th, for example, guarantee the right to vote regardless of race and gender respectively. The 13th outlawed slavery. The 18th (prohibition) was repealed by the 21st.

A2 The 14th Amendment's promise of equal protection under the law added to the legal guarantees offered under the Bill of Rights. The Bill of Rights made no mention of voting rights, so amendments have helped here too.

A3 The Equal Rights Amendment (see Card 10) was proposed but not ratified. Others have failed at the proposal stage, e.g. the Balanced Budget Amendment.

***examiner's* note** Commenting on the importance of amendments ratified since 1791 could really make your answers stand out.

Constitutional sources

UK/US comparative

Q1 Identify the sources of the UK and US Constitutions.

Q2 In what respects does US statute (passed through Congress) have a different status from UK statute law (passed through Parliament)?

Q3 How important a role is played by common law in each country?

ANSWERS

the origins of the UK and US Constitutions

A1 The US Constitution is *codified*. This document, including the various amendments and Supreme Court rulings that clarify its meaning, is the basis of US constitutional law. The UK Constitution is *uncodified*. It is based in statute, common law, conventions, works of authority and EU treaties and law.

A2 US statute is subject to the Constitution. Judicial review can declare it void. The UK Parliament is sovereign. Its statutes are the supreme source of constitutional law and cannot be declared unconstitutional.

A3 Common law is based on legal precedents (case law), a key source of constitutional law in both the UK and USA (see Card 51).

***examiner's* note** US constitutional law is as reliant upon Supreme Court interpretations of the constitution as it is on the document itself.

 **13** **ANSWERS**

Constitutional principles

UK/US comparative

Q1 How do the principles underlying the US Constitution differ from those upon which the UK Constitution rests?

Q2 Where is sovereignty in the UK and US systems?

Q3 To what extent is the US still a federal system and the UK still a unitary system?

ANSWERS

A1 In the UK, parliamentary sovereignty, the unitary state, parliamentary government under a constitutional monarchy and the rule of law are all key principles. The rule of law is also a key tenet of the US Constitution, but other principles (e.g. constitutional sovereignty, federalism) differ.

A2 In the USA, sovereignty is said to lie with the people under the US Constitution. In the UK, Parliament is said to be sovereign.

A3 US federal and state government roles remain distinct and cannot be taken away without constitutional amendment. Moves towards devolution have not made the UK federal, since Parliament retains the power to reverse any changes, through some speak of quasi-federalism.

***examiner's* note** Constitutional principles are rarely explicit in any constitutional settlement but may be visible through the way the political system operates.

Achieving constitutional change

Q1 How do the formal processes for changing the UK and US Constitutions differ?

Q2 How important a role is played by the UK and US judiciaries in bringing about changes in their respective constitutions through their powers of interpretation?

Q3 Is it more difficult to achieve constitutional change in the UK or in the USA?

ANSWERS

A1 The UK Constitution is changed easily by parliamentary statute, e.g. House of Lords Act, 1999. In the USA, constitutional changes require 'supermajorities' for proposal and ratification (see Card 10).

A2 The US Supreme Court's power of judicial review allows it to set the meaning of the Constitution through interpretation. This amounts to constitutional change in some cases. The UK courts do not have the same power because statute is the supreme constitutional law.

A3 The process of formal amendment (in the USA) is more difficult than passing a statute (in the UK). However, the role of US courts has meant that the US Constitution is less rigid than it might appear.

***examiner's* note** You need to understand informal as well as formal ways of effecting constitutional change.

(15) ANSWERS

Composition of the legislature

Q1 How is each US legislative chamber composed?

Q2 How are congressional elections organised?

Q3 Why are there two senators per state regardless of the size of each state?

ANSWERS

A1 Congress is divided into two chambers: the House of Representatives (House) and the Senate. The House consists of 435 members, apportioned between states on the basis of population. Each state has two senators.

A2 Senators serve a 6-year term, with one third being elected every 2 years. This is part of a system of staggered elections put in place to prevent a populist landslide victory. The whole House is elected every 2 years.

A3 The decision to give each state two senators was part of the Connecticut Compromise (see Card 6) and reflected the concerns of smaller states. It offered a balance to the more proportional House.

***examiner's* note** The system of staggered elections entrenched in the Constitution has often led to 'divided government' (see Card 23).

Resemblance theory

Q1 Is the membership of the US legislature representative of the US population in terms of ethnicity?

Q2 Is the membership of the US legislature representative of the US population economically?

Q3 How well are women represented in the House and the Senate?

ANSWERS))

theory of representation which argues that legislators should be typical of the communities they serve

A1 Of the US population in 2009, 12.4% was black and yet only 41 House members (9.4%) and one senator were black. Other races were similarly 'under' and in some cases 'un' represented.

A2 Most House members and senators are well-educated professionals (95% of those in Congress had a degree in 2009 and 38% had legal backgrounds).

A3 Although the number of women in Congress has risen since the 1970s, they are still under-represented (only 17.5% of House members and 17% of senators were women in 2009).

***examiner's* note** Most would agree that the US legislature should be more socially representative of the population as a whole. In 2009 the only black senator was Roland Burris (Illinois) and he was appropriated (i.e. not elected) to replace Barrack Obama in the chamber from 2009.

 **ANSWERS**

Constituency pressure

Q1 What is meant by constituencies in the US context?

Q2 Why do House members have to be more responsive to their constituents than senators?

Q3 Give an example of the ways in which members of Congress try to serve their constituents.

ANSWERS

pressure on members of the US Congress to serve the 'folks back home'

A1 A constituency is the district within a state that a House member is elected to represent. The smallest states have only one district, whereas larger ones have many more. Each senator is elected by the whole state.

A2 House members face a 'permanent campaign', with elections every 2 years and preparations for primaries starting almost as soon as they are sworn in. They represent a distinct district within a state so constituents tend to turn to them rather than to senators. Their voting records are subject to intense public scrutiny.

A3 They gain 'pork' (federal contracts and other benefits) for their states.

***examiner's* note** Congressmen must balance the concerns of constituents against the needs of those who backed them financially in their campaign (see Card 96).

 ANSWERS

Powers of the House

Q1 Distinguish between the powers the Constitution assigns to the House exclusively and those that are granted concurrently (jointly) with the Senate.

Q2 Why was the House granted a 'financial privilege'?

Q3 To what extent can the House resist pressure from the executive?

ANSWERS

constitutional powers of the House of Representatives, as clarified by convention and the Supreme Court

A1 The House has sole power to impeach members of the executive, including the president (e.g. Clinton). It also has a financial privilege in that it considers all money bills first. The House and Senate hold co-equal legislative power and must act jointly to declare war.

A2 It was given control over taxation as it was the only elected chamber until 1913. It is also more representative of state populations.

A3 House members are often reluctant to oppose a popular president for fear of losing their seats. The House can, however, be a significant obstacle, e.g. over Clinton's 1995 budget (see Card 23) or Obama's 2009 healthcare plan.

***examiner's* note** Presidents have often used public support to bully the chamber into submission, particularly in the foreign policy sphere (see Card 32).

(19) ANSWERS

Powers of the Senate

Q1 What powers are held by the Senate alone?

Q2 Identify ways in which the Senate is different from the House.

Q3 What is a filibuster?

constitutional powers held by the Senate, as opposed to those held concurrently with the House

A1 The Constitution grants the Senate sole power to try individuals who have been impeached. Most presidential appointments must also be confirmed by the Senate. The chamber has a unique foreign policy role, with all treaties requiring ratification by a $\frac{2}{3}$ Senate majority.

A2 The Senate's small membership means that there is more time for debate than in the House. Senators are more likely to hold positions of responsibility.

A3 A filibuster is where one or more senators decide to speak at length in order to prevent a measure being passed. Filibusters can only be ended by a cloture motion, requiring support of $\frac{3}{5}$ of the Senate.

examiner's note The chamber's sole powers are not merely theoretical. It has rejected presidential appointments and treaties, e.g. the Versailles Treaty in 1920.

Oversight of the executive

Q1 In what areas — besides legislation — does Congress oversee executive actions?

Q2 How much of a theoretical check does Congress provide over executive-inspired legislation?

Q3 To what extent can the president work around congressional oversight of his legislative proposals?

ANSWERS

the means by which the legislative branch can check executive actions, known as scrutiny in the UK

A1 The Senate has oversight of all key presidential appointments and treaties. Committees in both chambers (see Card 24) scrutinise the work of executive bodies.

A2 All legislative power is vested in Congress. The president has no formal input beyond making recommendations in the State of the Union Address and choosing whether to exercise his power of veto.

A3 The president can normally find Congress members to sponsor his bills. He can also mobilise public support against an obstructive Congress. Success rates, however, vary (see Card 33).

***examiner's* note** Some have argued that oversight became more effective after Watergate. In reality, however, measures such as the Case Act (1972) and the War Powers Act (1973) gave the president unconstitutional powers.

 (21) ANSWERS

Leadership in Congress

Q1 Who are the key congressional leaders?

Q2 What role is played by the speaker of the House of Representatives?

Q3 How powerful are party whips within the US Congress?

ANSWERS

A1 The key figures in the House are the speaker and the majority and minority leaders. Senate majority and minority leaders are also important. The role of Senate 'speaker' is less significant, being performed by the president *pro tempore* in the vice-president's absence.

A2 The House speaker is a 'player' rather than an 'umpire', referring bills to committee, appointing some committee chairs and the majority party contingent on the House Rules Committee (see Card 24). The speaker presides over the House, enforcing the rules.

A3 Whips may influence those within their party but have few means with which to court or threaten potential rebels.

***examiner's* note** Weak leadership is due to the relative weakness of parties, caused by factors such as the separation of powers.

 ANSWERS

Divided government

Q1 Identify two causes of divided government.

Q2 What is said to be the main consequence of divided government?

Q3 Is divided government necessarily a 'bad thing'?

ANSWERS

A1 The executive and legislative branches are elected separately, and elections for House, Senate and president are staggered, making it hard for one party to capture both branches. This is compounded by split-ticket voting (see Card 74).

A2 Gridlock can occur when the legislature and executive reach a stalemate over a legislative proposal (e.g. Clinton's 1995 Budget).

A3 It could be seen as a good thing if it leads to a more cooperative approach. After 1995, for example, Clinton had more success with the Republican-controlled Congress because he set more realistic goals and offered compromises.

***examiner's* note** Even when government is not divided, the president can face serious opposition from the legislature, e.g. Obama over his 2009 healthcare plan or Clinton over healthcare in 1993/94.

Congressional committees

Q1 Identify the roles performed by the various House and Senate committees.

Q2 What powers and resources do US standing committees have?

Q3 How important is the role played by standing committee chairs?

Q4 Why is the House Rules Committee so important?

ANSWERS ▶▶

the standing, select and other committees that exist in both House and Senate

A1 Standing committees are permanent and have legislative and oversight functions. Select committees are usually set up for more specific purposes and are not permanent. Conference committees resolve conflicts between House and Senate versions of bills.

A2 They have the power to amend and even kill bills (by pigeonholing them) and have the power of subpoena.

A3 Chairs prioritise bills, set the agenda and organise subcommittees. They are often courted by the executive.

A4 It is responsible for timetabling bills and assigning them a 'rule' that determines how vulnerable they are to amendment.

***examiner's* note** The status of standing committees is reflected in the fact that they consider bills *before* the second reading (unlike in the UK).

Composition of legislatures

UK/US comparative

Q1 Compare the composition of the 'lower chambers' in the UK and US legislatures.

Q2 Why and in what ways do UK and US second chambers differ in their composition?

Q3 To what extent do the members of the US and the UK legislatures resemble their respective populations?

ANSWERS

bicameral legislatures are common to both the USA and UK and many of the larger Western democracies

A1 The US House consists of 435 members, one elected per district in each state. The UK Commons consists of 650 members, each representing a parliamentary constituency. Each House member represents over 500,000 constituents; each MP represented around 67,000 in 2010.

A2 The Senate is an elected chamber of 100 members, two per state. The Lords in June 2010 was a largely appointed chamber of 707 peers. Peers have no constituencies.

A3 Neither US legislators nor those in the UK resemble the broader population they serve, being predominantly white, well-educated, middle-class, middle-aged men.

***examiner's* note** In federal bicameral systems, it is common for the second chamber to represent the various states on an equal rather than on a proportional basis.

(25) **ANSWERS**

Distribution of power within legislatures

UK/US comparative

Q1 Briefly compare the power of the UK and US second chambers.

Q2 Explain why the Senate and the Lords have such different roles.

Q3 Why is the US Senate often seen as being more prestigious than the House of Representatives?

ANSWERS ▶▶

the way legislative power is distributed between the two chambers is different in the USA and UK

A1 The Senate holds coequal legislative power with the House; the Lords' power is limited by devices such as the parliament acts. The Senate can also check the US executive through its role in confirming appointments and ratifying treaties.

A2 The limited powers of the UK Lords reflect the revising role of the chamber and its unelected status. The Senate's coequal legislative power reflects the system of presidential democracy and the fact that the chamber now has its own electoral mandate.

A3 The Senate's exclusive powers add to its prestige, as does its limited size and the more testing qualifications for office.

***examiner's* note** The powers of each second chamber reflect their respective roles. A move towards a fully elected Lords would lead to calls for coequal power.

Scrutiny of executive power

UK/US comparative

Q1 What methods of scrutinising the executive are common to both the UK and US systems of government?

Q2 How crucial to the scrutiny of the executive is a separation of powers?

Q3 Identify two reasons why congressional committees are more effective in their scrutiny of the executive than their UK counterparts.

ANSWERS

both UK and US legislatures have a role in scrutiny (often called 'oversight' in the USA) of the executive

A1 Both legislatures scrutinise their executives through debates, questions and committees.

A2 In the UK, scrutiny is made more difficult by the fusion of executive and legislative branches. Government control of a Commons majority, strong party ties and the effectiveness of party whips make checks less effective. In the USA, separation of powers, divided government, weak parties and feeble whipping can destroy the executive's agenda.

A3 US committees have access to greater resources than their UK equivalents, and have the power to subpoena witnesses.

***examiner's* note** It is not always the case that the US executive faces more effective scrutiny than in the UK. George W. Bush was given free rein in the wake of 9/11, while Tony Blair faced determined opposition, despite a massive Commons majority.

 **(27) ANSWERS**

Constitutional position

Q1 What kind of chief executive did the Founding Fathers intend the president to be?

Q2 What powers does the Constitution explicitly assign to the president?

Q3 What roles are implied?

A1 The Founding Fathers sought to limit the power of the executive to avoid tyranny. Yet, by adopting a presidential system, they showed their desire to create a single leader.

A2 The president has the power to appoint executive officers with the advice and consent of the Senate. He is also commander-in-chief of the armed forces, and has the power to sign or veto legislation and to address Congress.

A3 The State of the Union Address has seen the president become 'chief legislator', even though he cannot introduce bills. The role of head of state has also developed (see Card 30).

examiner's note The Founding Fathers gave the president no 'emergency power' but allowed enough 'wiggle-room' in the Constitution for him to act in times of need.

Limitations on
presidential power

Q1 Identify the key constitutional checks that operate on the powers of the president.

Q2 How effective are these checks in practice?

Q3 Outline one informal check on presidential power.

ANSWERS ▶▶

presidential power is limited by the checks and balances built into the US Constitution

A1 The president relies on Congress to introduce and pass his proposals. He can veto bills, but this can be overridden with a 2–3 majority in each chamber. Presidential nominees for key positions are subject to Senate confirmation and treaties require Senate ratification. While the president is commander in chief, Congress has the power to declare war.

A2 A popular president can mobilise public pressure against an obstructive Congress. Congress and the Supreme Court are often unwilling to stand up to the president in times of national emergency.

A3 Public opinion can be an effective check for a first-term president seeking re-election.

***examiner's* note** A popular and charismatic president (e.g. Clinton or Obama) can often circumvent many of the checks.

Growth of presidential power

Q1 Identify three factors that have led to a growth in presidential power.

Q2 Give two examples of the ways in which Congress has tried to limit this expansion of presidential power.

Q3 Is this growth in executive power irreversible?

ANSWERS))

the expansion of the powers of the US president in response to national and worldwide developments

A1 The expansion of the USA, the development of its world role, particularly militarily and economically, and the rise of the mass media have all enhanced the US president's role. The need for speed in modern warfare also favours a single leader.

A2 The Case Act (1972) and the War Powers Act (1973) tried to limit the president's use of 'executive agreements' and 'presidential wars' respectively.

A3 Many of the factors that have led to a growth in the president's power are irreversible. However, specific situations may make a president appear less powerful than his predecessors, e.g. divided government.

***examiner's* note** Although it is said that the balance of power swings between president and Congress, in reality, over time, it has favoured the executive.

 30 ANSWERS

Imperial or imperilled?

Q1 What were the key elements of Arthur Schlesinger's 'imperial presidency' thesis?

Q2 Why did Gerald Ford have a different view of the balance of power between president and Congress from Schlesinger?

ANSWERS ››

two contrasting interpretations of US presidential power from different historical contexts

A1 In *The Imperial Presidency* (1973), Arthur Schlesinger wrote of a gradual expansion of presidential power since ratification of the Constitution. He charted how presidents had used 'executive agreements' and undeclared 'presidential wars' to circumvent constitutional checks, and criticised Congress and the Supreme Court for failing to do their duties.

A2 In 1980 Gerald Ford (president 1974–77) criticised the Case Act (1972) and the War Powers Act (1973) as part of a process by which Congress intended to render the president powerless. Ford followed Nixon, was unelected, and faced a hostile Congress; Schlesinger was writing at the height of presidential power.

***examiner's* note** Both of these interpretations of the office of president must be read in context and are very much 'of their time'.

Two presidencies

Q1 What factors have allowed the president a greater freedom in foreign affairs than in the domestic sphere?

Q2 To what extent can Aaron Wildavsky's thesis from *The Two Presidencies* (1969) be applied to recent presidencies?

ANSWERS ▶▶

Wildavsky's thesis that a 'domestic policy president' is weaker than a 'foreign policy president'

A1 The Constitution divided domestic powers between legislature and executive far more clearly than it did foreign policy powers. Successful modern foreign policy is, by its nature, difficult to formulate in a legislature numbering 535 individuals.

A2 Clinton struggled to achieve his goals in domestic policy yet was seen as a success on the international stage. Bush's success in the Gulf War contrasted with his problems in domestic policy. In foreign affairs, George W. Bush was given virtual free rein post-9/11, but he still struggled to impose his domestic agenda. Obama did secure his healthcare reform.

***examiner's* note** In 2004, Democrats accused George W. Bush of manipulating the level of terrorist threat, creating a false emergency that made it hard for Congress to block his domestic and foreign policies for fear of appearing un-American. This is known as the president 'wrapping himself in the flag'.

Recent presidencies

Q1 How successful have recent presidents been in their dealings with Congress?

Q2 What factors account for differences in congressional success rates?

Q3 Identify one way in which George W. Bush's foreign policy has differed from that of his predecessors and account for this difference.

ANSWERS ▶▶

A1 Success rates vary between presidents and from year to year within presidencies. Clinton achieved 86% success in 1993, but 38% in 1999.

A2 The abilities of the incumbent president and of congressional leaders are important, as is the make-up of Congress. Divided government often leads to congressional obstruction. George W. Bush's success rate in 2001–03 was bolstered by the state of emergency post-9/11.

A3 Many presidents since the 1970s have been reluctant to engage in major military action due to the danger of getting bogged down — the 'Vietnam factor'. George W. Bush bucked this trend by adopting a more proactive foreign policy after 9/11.

examiner's note Presidents often have to modify their 'ideal foreign policy' to meet the demands of the time.

The vice-president

Q1 How are vice-presidents chosen?

Q2 What formal and informal roles does the vice-president play?

Q3 In what circumstances may the vice-president take over from the president?

ANSWERS ▶▶

the other half of the 'ticket' elected each presidential election

A1 Candidates are normally announced by the presidential candidates. If an incumbent vice-president dies, resigns or becomes president, the president may appoint a replacement, subject to confirmation by Congress.

A2 The vice-president has the role of 'first reserve' if the president is 'incapable' (see below). He is also president of the Senate, although the president *pro tempore* normally acts as chair.

A3 The vice-president becomes president on the president's death or resignation. Under the 25th Amendment, he may take over if the president declares himself unable to discharge his duties or if the vice-president and the majority of the cabinet believe he is unable to do so.

***examiner's* note** Though often ridiculed, the office of vice-president has undergone a renaissance in recent years.

Cabinet

Q1 Give two reasons why the US cabinet lacks status.

Q2 How often do cabinet meetings occur?

Q3 From what fields are cabinet members drawn?

ANSWERS

consists of the heads of the 15 executive departments plus agency heads and other key figures

A1 The cabinet has no constitutional basis as a collective body. The president is under no obligation to hold cabinet meetings or to listen to or act on the advice of his cabinet.

A2 Presidents such as Kennedy rarely held meetings. Others such as Reagan held almost weekly meetings, initially at least.

A3 They are not allowed to be serving members of the legislature. They are normally drawn from the ranks of former Congress members, serving or former state governors and academics. They are mostly policy specialists.

examiner's note The US cabinet has no collective responsibility. Its unelected members are not united by a campaigning experience or by party loyalty. Members answer only to the president and Congress for their departments.

The Executive Office of the President (EOP or EXOP)

Q1 What roles are played by the various bodies that constitute EOP?

Q2 Identify one reason why EOP has grown so rapidly since the 1930s.

Q3 Give an example of EOP being more of a hindrance to the president than a help.

ANSWERS

includes the White House Office, the
National Security Council and the
Office of Management and Budget

A1 The White House Office consists of the president's closest aides
and is coordinated by a chief of staff. The Office of Management
and Budget collates the budget. The National Security Council
coordinates domestic and foreign policy relating to national
security.

A2 Following the expansion of federal government intervention at
the time of the New Deal, the Brownlow Committee (1937)
concluded that 'the president needs help'. The EOP was
expanded to meet this need.

A3 Nixon became isolated as a result of his over-reliance on Bob
Haldeman, his chief of staff.

examiner's **note** Most presidents enter office with an explicit commitment
to reduce the size of EOP, but few are able to identify which posts are
expendable. EOP has, therefore, grown steadily since the 1930s.

The federal bureaucracy

Q1 Outline the scale of the federal bureaucracy.

Q2 Identify the functions performed by the federal bureaucracy.

Q3 Identify two or more problems that arise from the function of executive agencies and independent regulatory commissions.

ANSWERS ▶▶

the administration system that carries out government policy

A1 It consists of 15 executive departments, plus independent executive agencies, independent regulatory commissions (IRCs) and government corporations. In 2006 it had a payroll of nearly $14 billion and a staff of over 2.7 million.

A2 It oversees the execution of policy, establishes rules and regulations within the legislative framework and ensures that rules are enforced.

A3 Agencies and IRCs can fall victim to 'agency capture' (clientelism), where they end up serving the interests of those that they should be regulating. The emergence of iron triangles (see Card 96) can also result in agencies failing to carry out their duties effectively.

***examiner's* note** IRCs have been described as the 'headless fourth branch' of US government, owing to their quasi-legislative and quasi-judicial roles.

 ANSWERS

President and prime minister

Q1 What roles do the US president and the UK prime minister have in common?

Q2 How do their constitutional positions differ?

Q3 Which chief executive is the most powerful in relation to his/ her respective legislature?

ANSWERS

the UK and US 'chief executives' have many roles in common but fundamental differences exist

A1 Both have roles in patronage, agenda setting and foreign policy.

A2 The president's powers are enumerated in the Constitution. The prime minister's powers rest in part on his/her use of the monarch's prerogative powers. The president is granted the right to conclude treaties, with $\frac{2}{3}$ Senate approval, whereas the prime minster signs treaties on the monarch's behalf.

A3 The president's enumerated powers and independent election give certain advantages, but there are entrenched checks. The prime minister normally has a Commons majority and can exercise the prerogative powers, but he/she relies on the confidence of Parliament and party.

***examiner's* note** Comparisons of the relative power of prime minister and president are only meaningful in the context of their respective systems.

Cabinets

Q1 Identify key differences in the nature and power of the UK and US cabinets.

Q2 How similar are the processes by which cabinet members are chosen in each system?

Q3 Outline some ways in which the composition of the UK cabinet differs from its US counterpart.

ANSWERS

the US cabinet is different from the UK cabinet in composition, roles and power

A1 The UK cabinet was traditionally seen as a policy-making body, though this role has declined in recent years. The US cabinet has only as much influence as the president, who holds sole executive power, allows it.

A2 In both systems, the chief executive puts forward an individual. The US president's nomination is subject to Senate confirmation. The UK prime minister's nominee is formally appointed by the monarch.

A3 The UK cabinet consists largely of elected MPs, often generalists. In the USA, members of the legislature are barred from the executive and cabinet members tend to be specialists.

***examiner's* note** The UK cabinet is said to have declined as the power of the prime minister has increased. Blair's decision to hold fewer cabinet meetings and his reliance on bilaterals was reminiscent of the way in which many presidents have operated.

Executive branches

UK/US comparative

Q1 Identify a parallel between bodies within the UK core executive and its equivalent in the USA.

Q2 Assess the role of 'special advisors' (aides) in each country.

Q3 How important a role is played by the 'chief of staff' in each country?

ANSWERS ▶▶

unelected individuals and bodies who work under the chief executive, advising on the detail of policy

A1 There are parallels between EXOP (see Card 36) and the UK Cabinet Office. The strengthening of the latter since 1997, and the relocation of 17 of its offices to Downing Street, has effectively created a 'prime minister's department'.

A2 There were 69 special advisors by the end of New Labour's first year in office (1997), appointed to lessen reliance on the civil service and to keep tabs on departments. In the USA, the numbers of presidential aides soared in the 1930s. Some have played key roles.

A3 The US chief of staff coordinates the activities of the White House Staff. Blair was the first to use the title in the UK, awarding Jonathon Powell the role after 1997.

***examiner's* note** In the UK, the rise of special advisors has undermined the Cabinet.

40 ANSWERS

The system of US courts

Q1 Identify the various types of state courts that exist in the USA.

Q2 What kinds of cases do the various types of federal courts below the Supreme Court hear?

Q3 Where does the US Supreme Court fit into this system?

ANSWERS

the US court system comprises state and federal courts

A1 Most state cases are dealt with in State Trial Courts. They may be passed to the State Intermediate Court of Appeal and on to the State Supreme Court of Appeal (where a state has one).

A2 The 94 US District Courts deal with most cases involving federal statutes, the Constitution or large sums of money. There is also a US Claims Court and a US Court of International Trade. Appeals go to the appropriate US Court of Appeal.

A3 The US Supreme Court is the highest court of appeal for federal cases and for state cases that have exhausted the appeals process and have some bearing on the Constitution.

***examiner's* note** Do not confuse state supreme courts with the US Supreme Court (federal law/Constitution).

Supreme Court appointment and composition

Q1 Who determines the size of the Supreme Court?

Q2 Outline the process by which Supreme Court justices are appointed.

Q3 How 'political' is this process?

Q4 How representative of the broader US population is the current Supreme Court's membership?

ANSWERS ▶▶

the Supreme Court has had nine justices since the 1869 Judiciary Act

A1 Congress controls the size of the Supreme Court.

A2 The president nominates a justice when a vacancy arises. This nominee is then subject to judicial committee hearings before the Senate votes — a majority is needed for confirmation.

A3 Presidents try to ensure their nominees share their view on key issues. Confirmation may become politicised if the nominee holds views that are at odds with the Senate majority, e.g. the Senate's rejection of Reagan's nomination of the conservative Bork in 1987.

A4 In June 2010 women were under-represented (2/9). Black Americans (12.9% of the population) were more fairly represented (1/9).

***examiner's* note** The Court's membership, reflecting those reaching senior positions in the legal profession, is unlikely to be fully representative.

Supreme Court power

Q1 What does the Constitution say about the power of the Supreme Court?

Q2 What types of cases does the Supreme Court consider?

Q3 What is judicial review?

Q4 When was the power of judicial review first established?

A1 It gives it the power to hear cases involving public officials, or where a state is a party, directly. In all other cases, it acts as the highest court of appeal. (See also Card 41.)

A2 It considers cases where disputes have arisen between states, where state courts disagree, where state courts or law conflict with federal courts or law, or where a state court contradicts a Supreme Court ruling.

A3 It is the convention whereby the Court may void actions or statutes it considers to be in conflict with the Constitution.

A4 It was first used in the case of *Marbury v. Madison* (1803).

***examiner's* note** The Founding Fathers were deliberately vague about the extent of the Court's power. The development of judicial review has been crucial (see Card 44).

(43) ANSWERS

Judicial review, activism and restraint

Q1 What do you understand by the terms 'strict constructionist' and 'loose constructionist'?

Q2 Which period of the Supreme Court's history is most associated with the term 'judicial activism'?

Q3 Identify an example of the Court demonstrating 'restraint'.

ANSWERS ❯❯

the extensive and controversial use of judicial review (judicial activism) compared to its restrained use

A1 Strict constructionists favour a conservative, literal interpretation of the Constitution; loose constructionists adopt a more liberal view, reading 'between the lines'.

A2 Under Chief Justice Earl Warren (in office 1953–69), the Court made extensive use of its power of judicial review, often in sensitive areas. This led to the term 'judicial activism'.

A3 A good example is the Court's continued reluctance to overturn *Roe v. Wade* (1973) — it has allowed limits on access to abortion, but has resisted states' attempts to ban it.

***examiner's* note** Even during periods of supposed judicial activism, the Court rarely makes decisions diametrically opposed to the wishes of president, Congress and the public. When it does (e.g. over the New Deal), it can come under acute pressure.

The Court and civil rights

Q1 Why was the *Brown v. Board of Education, Topeka* (1954) case so significant?

Q2 Explain what is meant by the terms 'bussing' and 'affirmative action'.

ANSWERS ▶▶

A1 The Brown case (1954) rested on the constitutionality of segregation in schools. The Court used new sociological research to show that segregation created inequalities and was, therefore, unconstitutional. This set a precedent, theoretically outlawing segregation in all areas.

A2 Bussing was introduced in the wake of *Swann v. Charlotte-Mecklenberg Board of Education* (1971): pupils of different ethnic backgrounds were 'bussed' to school in order to provide racially mixed schools in all areas. Affirmative action is the practice of discriminating positively in favour of groups that have traditionally been discriminated against.

***examiner's* note** Cases such as *Brown* (1954), *Brown II* (1955) and *Alexander v. Holmes County Board of Education* (1969) did not end segregation — they simply declared it unconstitutional (see Card 11 for more detail on the Bill of Rights).

The Court and the rights of the accused

Q1 Which elements of the Constitution have been used to protect the rights of the accused?

Q2 Outline the significance of the Miranda case (1966).

Q3 Identify two cases that demonstrate how the meaning of the Constitution has changed over time in this area.

ANSWERS ▶▶

A1 The 5th Amendment prohibits punishment without 'due process of law' and protects the accused against self-incrimination. The 6th promises a 'speedy and fair public trial, by an impartial jury'. The 8th forbids 'excessive bail', 'fines' and 'cruel and unusual punishment'.

A2 *Miranda v. Arizona* (1966) ruled that citizens must be read their rights on arrest. Failure to do so could render evidence gained inadmissible.

A3 *Harris v. New York* (1971) ruled that confessions taken in violation of the Miranda rule could be used for limited purposes. *Duckworth v. Eagan* (1989) stated that the exact wording from Miranda did not have to be used for a subsequent confession to be valid.

examiner's note From 1963, various cases gave the accused the right to legal counsel before and during a trial.

The Court and abortion

Q1 What was the legal status of abortion prior to *Roe v. Wade* (1973)?

Q2 What did the Roe verdict say, and on which elements of the Constitution was it based?

Q3 To what extent have subsequent cases seen a narrowing of the Roe verdict?

ANSWERS

the right to abortion has been established entirely through judicial review

A1 As it was not mentioned in the Constitution, the power to regulate abortion was retained by individual states under the 10th Amendment.

A2 Roe established the right to abortion but recognised that more regulation might be appropriate beyond the first 3 months of pregnancy. It was based on earlier cases, which had established a 'zone of privacy' by interpreting passages in the 4th, 9th and 14th Amendments.

A3 Roe has not been overturned but the Court has since limited its scope. In *Webster v. Reproductive Health Services* (1989), for example, the Court upheld Missouri's law banning abortions from state facilities and state employees from performing them.

***examiner's* note** Ronald Reagan hoped to overturn Roe by nominating Supreme Court justices who shared his opposition to abortion.

 **ANSWERS**

Perspectives on the Court

Q1 Give an example of a Supreme Court justice defending the role of the Court.

Q2 Identify a case where one of the Court's judgements was so different from existing laws and precedent that it appeared to amount to a legislative change.

Q3 How may the Court appear to have a quasi-legislative authority where no laws or precedents exist?

ANSWERS ▶▶

A1 According to Justice Arthur Goldberg: '...the Supreme Court, when it decides a new legal question, does not make illegal what was previously legal; it gives a final authoritative determination of whether an action was legal when it took place.'

A2 The difference in interpretation of the 14th Amendment between Plessy (1896) and Brown (1954) saw the Court turn through 180° on the legality of segregation.

A3 Where there are no laws and the Constitution is unclear, justices effectively 'make law' through interpretation, identifying 'penumbras' and delivering their written opinions.

***examiner's* note** The Court only accepts around 4% of cases seeking to be heard each year. These tend to have great constitutional significance, setting legal precedents.

Judicial independence of the Court

Q1 What checks operate on the power of the US Supreme Court?

Q2 Give an example of the Supreme Court acting independently against the wishes of president and Congress.

Q3 Give an example of the Court appearing to bow to political pressure.

ANSWERS ▶▶

A1 President and Congress exercise some control through the
appointment process. Congress also controls the Court's
size and appellate jurisdiction. The Court's tendency towards
restraint means that it could be seen as a check on itself.

A2 *Clinton v. City of New York* (1998) saw the Court declaring
Congress's decision to grant the president a 'line-item veto'
unconstitutional.

A3 In cases such as *NLRB v. Jones & Laughlin Steel Corp* (1937) the
Court gave support to key elements of Roosevelt's New Deal
programme, having earlier declared them unconstitutional. This
change of heart was generally seen to be a result of Roosevelt's
threat to 'pack the court'.

examiner's note This term is not to be confused with 'judicial impartiality',
which implies justices are able to make decisions free from personal bias.

49 ANSWERS

Appointment of senior judges

Q1 How are senior judges appointed in the UK?

Q2 Identify similarities and differences between the UK appointments process and that operating in the USA.

Q3 To what extent is the appointment of senior judges in both systems a political process?

ANSWERS ▶▶

Refers to justices of the US and UK Supreme Courts and those serving on the appeals courts below

A1 Most senior UK judges are appointed on the recommendation of the independent Judicial Appointments Commission (JAC). Members of the UK Supreme Court are nominated by an ad-hoc commission and confirmed by the monarch having been notified by the Lord Chancellor.

A2 The only real similarity is that there is a two-stage process involving 'nomination' and 'confirmation'.

A3 The appointment of US Supreme Court justices is undeniably a political process. The UK judicial appointments process is supposed to be meritocratic.

***examiner's* note** Prior to the Constitutional Reform Act (2005) senior UK judges were appointed by the monarch on the advice of the Lord Chancellor following 'secret soundings'.

 ANSWERS

Judicial review

UK/US comparative

Q1 In what respects is the meaning of judicial review different in the USA from in the UK?

Q2 Are there any circumstances in which the UK courts can strike down UK statute law?

Q3 Give an example of judicial review from each country.

ANSWERS

A1 In the USA, it is the Supreme Court's right to void actions, regulations, or laws where they are judged to violate the Constitution. In the UK, the supremacy of statute law means higher courts can normally only declare that someone has acted beyond their authority. They cannot question an Act.

A2 UK courts cannot void statute law (but see below).

A3 In the USA, the Brown case (1954) remains the best known. A recent UK example is the finding that David Blunkett had not acted *ultra vires* when moving to suspend a senior police officer.

***examiner's* note** Since 1990, British courts can suspend UK statutes if they appear to violate EU law, at least until the European Court of Justice has made a final determination. They can also issue 'declarations of incompatibility' under the Human Rights Act (1998).

 ANSWERS

Protecting rights

UK/US comparative

Q1 What kinds of rights are protected in each country?

Q2 Define the terms 'Bill of Rights' (USA) and 'Human Rights Act' (UK).

Q3 What is the legal difference between the US Bill of Rights and the UK Human Rights Act?

ANSWERS

A1 Both countries protect what might be considered core civil rights. These include the freedom of speech and worship, the right to assemble and protest, and the right to a free and fair public trial.

A2 In the USA, the Bill of Rights refers to the first ten amendments to the constitution. The Human Rights Act (HRA) incorporates most of the European Convention on Human Rights (ECHR) into British law.

A3 The Bill of Rights is entrenched and, as such, is superior to regular law. The HRA is a regular piece of statute and cannot be used to declare other statutes void.

examiner's **note** The ECHR is not a product of the EU. Neither it nor the HRA have the status of EU law.

Electoral systems

Q1 What electoral system is used in US federal elections?

Q2 By what means has the franchise been extended over time?

Q3 Briefly outline the part played by primary elections and caucuses in presidential elections.

ANSWERS

A1 Congressional elections operate under a first-past-the-post system. Candidates for any one of a state's house districts are elected with a margin of at least one vote. Senators are elected by securing a similar margin across the state as a whole. The president wins office by securing an overall majority of Electoral College votes (see Card 60).

A2 The franchise has been extended through Acts of Congress and by constitutional amendment (see Card 12).

A3 Primary elections and caucuses select delegates to represent each state party at their respective national nominating conventions (see Cards 55 and 56).

examiner's note Primaries are also often used in congressional elections to select each party's candidate.

(53) ANSWERS

Staggered elections

Q1 Why did the Founding Fathers adopt a system of staggered elections?

Q2 Briefly outline the way in which the election system operates.

Q3 Has this system delivered the benefits that the Founding Fathers anticipated?

ANSWERS

> a system whereby there is no single
> point at which the entire legislature
> and presidency are 'up for grabs'

A1 The Founding Fathers feared that democracy, unchecked, could result in mobocracy. It was partly this fear that led them to stagger elections in order to make it impossible for a single populist party to gain control of House, Senate and the White House on a single day.

A2 The House is elected every 2 years, as is a third of the Senate. The president is elected every 4 years, on the leap year.

A3 Staggered elections have made 'divided government' more likely, although factors such as split-ticket voting (see Card 74) have also contributed to this phenomenon.

examiner's **note** Although the staggered terms were entrenched, direct elections to the Senate were only introduced with the 17th Amendment (1913). Prior to that, senators were chosen by each state's legislature.

 54 ANSWERS

Caucuses

Q1 Briefly outline how caucuses operate.

Q2 Outline two arguments in favour of the use of caucuses over primaries in presidential elections.

Q3 Identify two main weaknesses of the caucus system as compared to the primary system in presidential elections.

ANSWERS ▶▶

meetings of local party activists, still used in some states as a means of selecting delegates

A1 In states that use caucuses in presidential elections, local meetings often feed up to state-wide caucuses which then send delegates to the national nominating conventions.

A2 A tiered system like caucuses makes sense in states with small, dispersed populations. Caucuses may favour less charismatic but able candidates.

A3 Primaries involve the broader public in candidate selection, whereas caucuses have been associated with party 'fat cats' in 'smoke-filled rooms'. Caucuses may also favour candidates who are popular among activists but unappealing to the public.

***examiner's* note** Although the first caucus (Iowa) occurs before the first primary (New Hampshire) in presidential election year, the latter generally has more status.

Presidential primaries

Q1 Identify one way in which primaries can differ from state to state.

Q2 What is the 'invisible primary'?

Q3 Why is the New Hampshire primary so important?

Q4 What is 'front-loading'?

ANSWERS

A1 Some states hold open primaries (voters can vote in either party's primary); others hold closed primaries (voters must be registered party supporters).

A2 It is the period between candidates declaring their intention to run and the start of the primary season proper. During this time candidates aim to raise money and gain recognition.

A3 It is the first. Despite being a small state with few delegates, the winner attracts media coverage and finance.

A4 This is where states schedule primaries early in the season to gain media attention and raise awareness of regional issues.

***examiner's* note** The rise in the use of primaries rather than caucuses since 1968 has diminished the formal roles of the national nominating conventions (see Card 57).

 **56 ANSWERS**

Party conventions

Q1 What formal roles do the national nominating conventions play?

Q2 How have these formal roles been eroded over time?

Q3 What informal roles do conventions perform?

ANSWERS ▶▶

the quadrennial national nominating conventions, at which delegates nominate their party's candidates

A1 They choose the party's 'ticket': their presidential and vice-presidential candidates. They approve the 'planks' that make up the party's 'platform' (its manifesto). They also elect a national committee to organise the next convention and to manage the party in the intervening period.

A2 The rise of primaries and 'committed delegates' has meant that the winning candidate is normally known before the convention starts. The 'platform' has also become less of an issue as campaigns have become more candidate-centred.

A3 Parties use modern conventions to raise campaign finance, court the media and present a unified front.

***examiner's* note** Conventions can go spectacularly wrong. The 1992 Republican convention was undermined by the quarrel between George Bush and Pat Buchanan.

 **ANSWERS**

Candidacy in US elections

Q1 What formal rules govern candidature in US congressional and presidential elections?

Q2 Outline two apparent informal barriers to presidential candidacy.

Q3 What kinds of people get elected to federal office in the USA?

ANSWERS

the criteria for candidacy in US congressional and presidential elections

A1 House candidates must be at least 25, US citizens for 7 years and residents of the state in which they are standing. Senate candidates must be at least 30, US citizens for 9 years and residents in their chosen state. Presidential candidates must have been born in the USA, be at least 35 and US residents for 14 years.

A2 Modern campaigns are expensive, requiring a personal fortune and/or good fundraising networks. Candidates also need to be charismatic and telegenic (e.g. Reagan, Clinton and Obama).

A3 Most are well-educated, white, Protestant men in their forties or older and from a professional background (see also Card 17).

***examiner's* note** The citizenship and residency requirements rule out a disproportionate number of non-white Americans.

The general election campaign

Q1 What are the main characteristics of the general election campaign?

Q2 Identify the main kinds of events that occur during this period.

Q3 Briefly outline issues surrounding the election day itself.

campaign between the end of the
convention season (August) and
presidential election day (November)

A1 It is characterised by intense media coverage. In recent years, there has been a rise in negative campaigning, including 'attack ads' (see Card 62).

A2 Candidates tour the USA, often focusing on key 'swing states'. Mass rallies allow them to tailor their message to the needs of each state and to attract valuable media coverage. Candidates also normally take part in televised debates with one another.

A3 The voting intentions of many are fixed by election day. Party workers focus more on 'getting the vote out' at this stage.

***examiner's* note** The Republicans held their 2004 convention directly after the Olympics, allowing them to have a very compact general election campaign. The Democrats had to hold their convention in July, before the Olympics; this threatened their campaign's momentum.

 **ANSWERS**

The Electoral College

Q1 Why was the Electoral College (EC) instituted?

Q2 How is the Electoral College constituted, and what does a presidential candidate need to do in order to be elected?

Q3 Outline two potential problems arising from the operation of the Electoral College.

ANSWERS ▶▶

the body that formally elects the president in the December of election year

A1 The Founding Fathers were unwilling to place too much power in the hands of voters.

A2 The EC has 538 members, each casting a single vote. The winning candidate needs to secure an overall majority (270/538) in order to become president. Each state's allocation is arrived at by adding together the number of senators and House members it has. Three additional electors represent Washington DC.

A3 Candidates may win the popular vote, yet lose the EC vote (e.g. Gore, 2000). A close race or a strong third-party candidacy can lead to a 'hung College', with no candidate achieving a majority.

***examiner's* note** It is not the state's *actual* House members and senators who vote in the College, but electors chosen specifically for the task.

Campaign finance

Q1 Identify three reasons why presidential campaigns are so expensive.

Q2 Give three sources of campaign finance.

Q3 What did the 1974 Federal Election Campaign Act (FECA) do?

Q4 What was meant by the term 'soft money'?

ANSWERS

A1 The size of the USA, the length of the campaign and an increasing reliance on paid media make campaigning expensive.

A2 Many candidates have personal fortunes (e.g. John Kerry and his wife). Candidates also get money from individual donors and from interest groups, via political action committees (PACs).

A3 The Act limited 'hard money', imposing a $1,000 limit on individual donations, although PACs (see Card 95) could donate up to $5,000.

A4 This was money given to parties to fund measures aimed at increasing voter registration and turnout. Not used directly on campaigns, it was exempted from the FECA in 1979. Abuse of this loophole prompted the Bipartisan Campaign Finance Reform Act (2002).

***examiner's* note** Both the 1974 and 2002 Acts faced Supreme Court review.

(61) ANSWERS

The role of the media

Q1 What rules, if any, control the political content of programmes broadcast on US television?

Q2 In what ways has the rise of the mass media increased the cost of US election campaigns?

Q3 Identify two ways in which the media have changed the nature of campaigns.

Q4 What are 'attack ads'?

ANSWERS

A1 US television is free from any UK-style legal requirement to remain impartial. Candidates can broadcast as many ads as they can afford to.

A2 Paid media are expensive. A typical 30-second local television ad can cost up to $1,000.

A3 The rise of the media has led to more telegenic candidates coming to the fore. It has also led to the emergence of 'sound-bite' politics, as lengthy discussion of policy detail is passed over.

A4 These are negative ads that seek to discredit an opponent. In 2004, individuals linked to George W. Bush's team produced ads discrediting John Kerry's record in Vietnam.

***examiner's* note** Television allows candidates to connect with more voters than was previously possible.

Congressional elections

Q1 When do congressional elections take place?

Q2 About what are congressional elections concerned?

Q3 Give a brief outline of a congressional race from the 2002 mid-term elections.

ANSWERS

A1 House elections take place every 2 years in November. They occur in presidential election years (leap years) and in the middle of each presidential term (mid-term elections). Senate elections also take place every 2 years, but only one third of the Senate is up for election each time.

A2 Congressional elections tend to be more focused on state issues and on the incumbent's voting record in Congress than on national issues.

A3 In 2010, incumbent liberal Democrat House member for California's 23 District, Lois Capps was unchallenged in the primary but faced a challenge from Republican Tom Watson in the November election. Capps was first elected to the House of Representatives in 1998, replacing her husband, who died suddenly in 1997.

***examiner's* note** Most House (94%) and Senate (87%) incumbents who sought re-election were re-elected in 2010.

 63 **ANSWERS**

Referendums, initiatives and recalls

Q1 Define the term referendum and give an example of how referendums have been used in one named state.

Q2 In what respect are initiatives different from referendums?

Q3 What do you understand by the term 'recall'?

ANSWERS ▶▶

A1 A referendum is a popular vote on a specific measure. Referendums generally take place when the legislature decides to, is required to, or is forced by public petition to put a measure to a public vote. In 2008 Californians passed Proposition 8; which barred same-sex marriages in the state.

A2 Initiatives, unlike referendums, allow voters to propose laws. They operate in 24 states, e.g. Proposition 13 (California, 1978).

A3 The recall device gives citizens the chance to remove and replace an elected office holder before the end of his/her term, e.g. the removal of Californian governor Gray Davis in 2003.

***examiner's* note** Critics argue that these devices create a tyranny of the majority. They could all be said to undermine representative democracy.

Electoral systems

UK/US comparative

Q1 Identify one strength and one weakness of the first-past-the-post system in the UK and the USA.

Q2 What impact does the system have on minor parties?

Q3 In what respect can we draw a parallel between the US Electoral College and the UK Parliament?

ANSWERS ▶▶

A1 In both countries the system normally results in a clear winner. On the negative side, it leads to a large number of wasted votes.

A2 It punishes them because their support is rarely sufficiently concentrated in any one area for them to win a contest outright.

A3 The presidential hopeful secures office once he has an overall majority of Electoral College (EC) votes. In the UK, the party leader effectively becomes prime minister elect as soon as his or her party has won an overall majority of Commons seats. In this sense, parallels may be drawn.

***examiner's* note** Some have suggested removing the EC and awarding the presidency to the candidate with the biggest share of the popular vote. It has also been argued that the UK prime minister should be elected independently.

 **65** ANSWERS

Candidate selection

UK/US comparative

Q1 What role do local US and UK political parties have in selecting the candidates who stand for elected office in their areas?

Q2 What input, if any, do national UK and US parties have over the process of candidate selection?

Q3 Which system of candidate selection brings the best candidates to the fore?

ANSWERS

UK-style party selection of candidates has been undermined in the USA by the rise of primaries

A1 Local parties in the USA have an increasingly limited role in candidate selection, largely due to the rise of primaries. UK constituency parties normally play a significant role, including short-listing candidates.

A2 In the UK, the Labour National Executive Council has the power to impose its own candidate over one selected by the constituency party (e.g. Shaun Woodward in St Helens). UK national parties also manage lists of approved candidates. US 'national parties' have no such role.

A3 US primaries encourage public participation, but the resulting candidate may not be the most capable politician. UK parties place more power with party members.

***examiner's* note** UK parties also have the power to deselect an individual — even a serving MP — as their candidate for the next election.

 **ANSWERS**

Referendums

Q1 What status is afforded to referendums within the US and UK systems of government?

Q2 How widespread has the use of referendums been in both countries?

Q3 Has the rise in the use of such mechanisms in both countries enhanced or undermined democracy?

ANSWERS

public votes on specific measures that have been passed or proposed by the government

A1 Although the US Constitution does not mention referendums and such devices are not used nationally, many states have used their reserved powers to add such procedures to their state constitutions. In the UK, referendums have been used to legitimise some constitutional changes.

A2 Eight referendums had been held in the UK by June 2010, although only one was UK wide (over EEC membership, 1975). They have been used more widely in the USA in recent years over issues as diverse as gay marriage and the legal status of cannabis.

A3 Some contend that referendums undermine representative democracy. Others say that they can help focus the mandate on some issues.

examiner's note Referendums are probably less controversial than initiatives or recalls (see Card 64).

(67) ANSWERS

Analysing US voting behaviour

Q1 Identify one model that can be applied to US voting behaviour.

Q2 Are primacy factors (e.g. income and occupation) or recency factors (e.g. issues and events) most important in determining the outcome of US elections?

Q3 How well does the voting context model explain US voting behaviour?

ANSWERS ▶▶

A1 The social structures model is applicable because there are links between variables such as occupation, income, education, geography, ethnicity, gender and voting.

A2 Some primacy factors have weakened over time, e.g. the Democrats have lost control of the 'Solid South'. Elections have become increasingly candidate- and issue-based, e.g. the economy in 2008.

A3 The voting context model holds that voting behaviour differs by type of election and over time. In the USA, for example, some voters 'split their tickets' (see Card 74) because they believe Republicans make better presidents and Democrats better House members.

***examiner's* note** Voting behaviour is made more volatile by the number of independent voters and ideological and political overlap.

Party identification in the USA

Q1 How strongly do US citizens identify with a particular political party?

Q2 Do these natural affiliations have a strong influence on an individual's voting behaviour?

Q3 Identify one reason why US voters might choose to vote for a party other than the one with which they are affiliated.

ANSWERS ▶▶

the proportion of US voters who support either the Republicans or the Democrats

A1 In 2008, 71% of voters identified with one of the two major parties (39% with the Democrats, 32% with the Republicans). Most of the rest regarded themselves as independent voters.

A2 In 2008, 89% of those who identified with the Democrats voted for Obama and 90% of Republican identifiers voted for John McCain.

A3 This might happen if the candidate of the opposing party has strong personal attributes or moves enough on policy to make the switch acceptable. In 1992, for example, many moderate Republicans were impressed by Clinton and his 'new Democrat' platform.

***examiner's* note** Since 74% of voters identified with a party in 2000, victory in presidential elections might be expected to go to the party that persuades more of its own supporters to remain loyal.

 **ANSWERS**

Ethnicity and voting in the USA

Q1 What proportion of the US population consists of ethnic minorities?

Q2 Is there a clear correlation between ethnicity and voting behaviour in the USA?

Q3 What measures have US political parties taken to gain support from ethnic minorities?

ANSWERS

the voting behaviour of the large ethnic minority population in the USA

A1 In 2009, 12.4% of the population was black, 4.4% Asian and 2.3% of mixed race; 15.4% was Hispanic or Latino, but there is overlap as Hispanics/Latinos may also be black.

A2 In 2008, 55% of white voters supported McCain; 95% of black voters, and 67% of Hispanics/Latinos favoured Obama.

A3 The Democrats have come to be seen as the party of ethnic minorities through their introduction of civil rights legislation and their link with large government welfare programmes. George W. Bush won support among Hispanics in 2000 and 2004 by targeting the group.

***examiner's* note** In the 1980s and 1990s black leaders such as Jesse Jackson sought to encourage electoral participation among ethnic minorities by voter-registration drives.

Gender and voting in the USA

Q1 To what extent is there a 'gender gap' in US presidential elections?

Q2 What factors might explain this gender gap?

Q3 Is registration and turnout higher among US women or men?

ANSWERS ▶▶

A1 Women favoured Democrats over Republicans in the 1992, 1996, 2000, 2004 and 2008 elections. In 2008, for example, women favoured Obama over McCain by 56%, as opposed to 43%, whereas amongst men the margin in favour of Obama was just 49% to 48%.

A2 Some have suggested that it is the result of the policies put forward by each party — the low tax, anti-abortion, pro-gun outlook of the Republicans being less attractive to women than the welfare provision, pro-choice and pro-gun-control stance associated with the Democrats.

A3 In 2008, 72.8% of women were registered and 65.7% voted, whereas the figures for men were 69.1% and 61.5% respectively.

***examiner's* note** At the 2010 UK General Election men voted 38% conservative and 28% labour while women voted 36% conservative and 31% labour.

 ANSWERS

Issue voting in the USA

Q1 What kinds of issues are weighty enough to influence the outcome of US elections?

Q2 Give an example of a recent election where an issue was said to have swung the result.

Q3 Give an example of a president trying to control and take advantage of the issues that emerge during a campaign.

ANSWERS

A1 Domestic issues are usually more influential than foreign policy ones. The state of the economy was a major influence on elections in the 1980s and early 1990s.

A2 The Democrats' successful 1992 campaign centred on George Bush's management of the US economy and in particular on Bush's unfulfilled 1988 election pledge 'Read my lips. No new taxes'.

A3 In the 2004 election George W. Bush's team, aware that Kerry's much decorated military career was giving him the upper hand as the Iraq situation deteriorated, encouraged those who sought to undermine Kerry's service record in Vietnam.

***examiner's* note** Some presidential candidates have benefited from taking a particular foreign policy stance (e.g. Eisenhower, 1952, 'I will go to Korea').

Turnout in the USA

Q1 What problems arise from the way in which turnout is calculated in the USA?

Q2 What do we mean by differential turnout?

Q3 Identify one factor which might explain low turnout in US congressional and presidential elections.

ANSWERS

A1 The use of VAP is problematic. Not all those of voting age are entitled to vote (for example, some are not US citizens). Others are entitled to vote but are not registered. Both factors mean any measurement of turnout by voting age is artificially low.

A2 This is when sections of the electorate or people from different regions display different levels of turnout from the headline figure.

A3 Many have attributed low turnout to a general disaffection with the political system, fed by a sense that democracy is serving special interests, not the public.

***examiner's* note** In recent years, some commentators have suggested that low turnout in US elections might be the result of 'hapathy' — where voters are happy with the way things are and do not feel the need to vote — rather than disaffection.

 ANSWERS

Split-ticket voting

Q1 Give an example of split-ticket voting.

Q2 Suggest three reasons why US voters might choose to 'split their tickets'.

Q3 Identify the main consequence(s) of 'split-ticket' voting.

ANSWERS

A1 Examples are numerous. In 2008, Democrat presidential candidate Barrack Obama won Indiana on the day that the state returned Republican Mitch Daniels as governor.

A2 Voters may be more concerned with the candidates' personal qualities or views than with their party labels. They may feel that 'Republicans make better presidents' and 'Democrats make better Congressmen'. Voters may wish to bring about 'divided government'.

A3 Divided government (see Card 23) is the most likely consequence of split-ticket voting. Another consequence might be that candidates place less emphasis on party during their campaign.

examiner's **note** Split-ticket voting is when voters split their support between candidates of different parties running for different offices on a *single* election day.

Non-electoral participation

Q1 Identify the range of activities that the term non-electoral participation might cover.

Q2 How fully do US citizens participate in political activities, other than voting?

ANSWERS

US forms of political participation other than electoral turnout

A1 Non-electoral participation might include membership of, or involvement in, campaigns set up by political organisations such as pressure groups. It might also take the form of direct involvement in the work of a political party — for example, working as a volunteer in the campaign office of a candidate or canvassing voters.

A2 Around 80% of Americans are said to be members of at least one pressure group. They are also 3.5 times *more* likely to be involved in the kind of campaign work that would normally be associated with grassroots party activists in the UK.

***examiner's* note** In recent years, many Western liberal democracies have seen a move away from more traditional forms of participation (e.g. voting) towards less traditional, non-electoral forms.

Recent election campaigns

Q1 What factors led to Clinton's victory in 1992?

Q2 What was the 'Contract with America'?

Q3 Which issues were important in the 2008 presidential election?

ANSWERS

A1 Clinton's victory in 1992 has often been attributed to George Bush's overemphasis on his foreign policy achievements, which allowed Clinton to stake a claim to the domestic agenda. Clinton's natural charisma also appealed to voters.

A2 The 'Contract' was the platform on which the Republicans fought the 1994 mid-term elections. It included a guarantee of a balanced budget and a commitment to the introduction of term limits.

A3 On-going US involvement in Afghanistan was a key issue, as was the state of the US economy.

***examiner's* note** The Republicans' success in the 1994 mid-terms, in which they won control of House and Senate, was as much a protest vote against Clinton as it was a positive vote for the 'Contract'.

Political culture

Q1 What are said to be the main elements of political culture in the UK?

Q2 To what extent are these key elements still relevant today?

Q3 These features do not apply in the USA. What are the main features of US political culture?

ANSWERS

defined by Lynton Robins as the
'citizenry's collective attitudes to the
political system and their role in it'

A1 UK political culture was traditionally said to be based on homogeneity, consensus and deference.

A2 Homogeneity has been eroded by factors such as immigration and the rise of Scottish and Welsh nationalism. The rise of nationalist parties in Scotland and Wales and the growth of the BNP have helped to undermine consensus. Deference has been undermined by an increasingly critical media.

A3 It is based on ideas such as liberty, limited government, individualism, a laissez-faire approach and belief in the 'American Dream'.

***examiner's* note** The concept of political culture implies that it is possible to generalise about the way in which things are likely to operate politically within a country as a whole. Regional differences undermine this approach.

Influences on voting

UK/US comparative

Q1 How much influence do primacy factors, such as income, occupation and class, have on voting?

Q2 Assess the importance of ethnicity as regards voting in both countries.

Q3 Are recency factors, such as issues and events, now more important than primacy factors in determining the outcome of UK and US elections?

ANSWERS

factors (e.g. ethnicity) common to both UK and US voting patterns and others that are country-specific

A1 Despite talk of class-dealignment, in the UK 2010 general election 39% of those in classes A/B voted for Conservatives (26% Labour) while 40% of those in classes D/E voted Labour (31% Conservatives). In the USA, the focus is more on occupation and income.

A2 Ethnic minorities tend to vote for the Democrats in the USA and for Labour candidates in the UK.

A3 Recency factors are said to have become more important due to the erosion of long-term factors that were once key (e.g. age, education, social class). Events can prove crucial, as can the relative qualities of candidates.

***examiner's* note** Strong party identification is in decline on both sides of the Atlantic, so short-term factors can have a significant impact on voter choice.

 **ANSWERS**

Turnout

UK/US comparative

Q1 What are the consequences of using different measures when comparing turnout in the UK and the USA?

Q2 How does turnout in the UK compare with that in the USA?

Q3 Does turnout vary between different types of elections?

ANSWERS ▶▶

A1 The US measure results in artificially low figures because some of those who are of voting age are ineligible and/or unregistered.

A2 The headline figures suggest that US turnout is lower than that in the UK (58.2% in the 2008 presidential election compared to 65.1% in the 2010 UK general election). If, however, the UK measure (i.e. percentage of registered voters) were applied, the US figure for 2008 would be 90%.

A3 Yes. In the 2009 European elections, the UK turnout was only 34.5%. In the USA, turnout at congressional elections is around 15% lower in the mid-terms than in presidential election years.

***examiner's* note** 'Motor voter' measures in the USA and experiments in postal, text and e-mail voting in the UK have increased turnout.

The US party system

Q1 What factors favoured the emergence of a two-party system in the USA?

Q2 Identify the main arguments for and against the view that the USA is a two-party system.

Q3 To what extent do the two main parties dominate major elected office?

ANSWERS ▶▶

the party system of the USA — like that of the UK — is now generally regarded as a 'two-party system'

A1 This has been brought about by the need for a clear choice between candidates under a first-past-the-post system, and the fact that certain issues have polarised US opinion through time (e.g. slavery).

A2 The vast majority of elected politicians represent one of the two major parties. However, some argue that there are in fact 51 unique party systems: one in Washington DC and one in each of the 50 states.

A3 All but two Congress members and all but 1 of 50 state governors belonged to one of the two major parties in June 2010, as have all presidents since 1853.

***examiner's* note** The phrase 'two-party system' suggests that the two parties are distinct and ideologically coherent organisations. However, members of a party from one state often have little in common politically with those from another.

US parties: origins and rise

Q1 How did the Founding Fathers view political parties, and what did they do in order to limit the extent to which parties could dominate the US system of government?

Q2 Identify two factors that led to the rise of US political parties.

Q3 What is meant by the term 'machine politics'?

ANSWERS

the factions present at ratification of the US Constitution subsequently evolved into distinct parties

A1 They were suspicious of political parties. Alexander Hamilton felt that the aim of the Constitution should be to establish a system of government under which 'no alliance of interests could ever gain control of the whole'. Power was fragmented by devices such as the separation of powers, checks and balances, and staggered elections.

A2 Parties offered a largely immigrant population something to belong to. In the absence of a welfare state, parties also came to offer a safety net for those facing hard times.

A3 The term refers to the almost total control secured by political parties in some cities by the 1950s.

examiner's note All powerful party machines were often highly focused and territorial.

 ANSWERS

Theories of US party decline

Q1 Identify two ways in which the growth of the federal government after 1930 led to a decline in the role of political parties.

Q2 Why has the increased use of primaries diminished the role of parties in elections?

Q3 How has the development of broadcast media undermined the role of US political parties?

ANSWERS

theories relating to the diminishing power and influence of US political parties

A1 The introduction of federal welfare programmes undermined the parties' role in providing a kind of 'safety net' at state or city level. Growth of both federal government and the country's world role has distanced the president from his party in Congress.

A2 Primaries took the key role of candidate selection out of the hands of committed party activists and placed it in the hands of the broader electorate.

A3 It has allowed candidates to nurture a direct relationship with voters, making them less reliant on the party machine during elections.

***examiner's* note** 'Machine politics' still exists in some areas although, as Anthony Bennett has noted, the days of the 'cigar chomping, fedora-hatted political boss' probably ended with the death of Mayor Richard Daley in 1976.

 **82** ANSWERS

US parties resurgent?

Q1 Why did the Democrats introduce super delegates at their conventions from 1984, and what are they?

Q2 Identify one way in which political parties have strengthened their national organisation in recent years.

Q3 How did the emergence of 'soft money' enhance the role of parties?

ANSWERS ▶▶

A1 Super delegates are normally elected officials or party elders. They were introduced to augment the influence of party loyalists relative to the delegates selected in primary elections. Of the delegates attending the 2008 Democratic Convention, 19.5% were super delegates.

A2 The national committees are now more permanent organisations, with offices in Washington DC and roles beyond organising the quadrennial party nominating conventions.

A3 The 1979 amendment to the Federal Election Campaign Act allowed parties to collect money for use in grassroots campaigns. This 'soft money' was restricted under the 2002 Act (see Card 61).

***examiner's* note** Much of the decline in political parties has been due to changes in US society and government and is, therefore, beyond party control.

Traditional US party ideologies and policies

Q1 Are US parties ideologically based?

Q2 What kinds of policies have traditionally been associated with the Democratic Party?

Q3 What kinds of policies have traditionally been associated with the Republicans?

ANSWERS))

US parties lack ideological distinctiveness but have traditionally had different priorities and policies

A1 As Richard Hofstadter noted, the USA's fate was 'not to have ideologies, but to be one'. Central to this 'ideology' — to which both main US political parties subscribe — is a belief in limited government, liberty and the 'American Dream'.

A2 Associated with 'big government' from the 1930s, Democrats have favoured higher spending on education and welfare. They have been more liberal on social policy (e.g. pro-choice) and more internationalist.

A3 Republicans have favoured less government intervention, lower taxation and lower public spending on education and welfare. They have been more conservative on social policy (e.g. pro-life) and more isolationist.

***examiner's* note** These are generalisations: some Democrats are pro-life and many 'new Democrats' believe the age of 'big government' is over (see Cards 85 and 86).

 **84** ANSWERS

US parties: ideological overlap

Q1 Outline one pressure that has led parties to move towards the political centre.

Q1 Identify an area or an issue on which parties now appear to agree.

Q2 On what issues, if any, do US parties remain divided?

ANSWERS

the tendency of both parties to drift towards the centre, marginalising their more extreme members

A1 Media coverage means that candidates often drop or play down policies that are likely to bring adverse media attention (e.g. George W. Bush's silence on the issue of abortion in 2000). Instead, they advocate policies that will appeal to all.

A2 Both parties appear to agree that the era of liberal 'big government' is over, though the election on Barrack Obama saw Republicans and Democrats in Congress dividing along party lines over healthcare and the economy.

A3 The real differences are now in 'tone' and 'degree'. Even on abortion, said to be the last big divide, there is overlap. Less than 10% of Republicans supported the party's proposed blanket ban at the 1992 party convention. Similarly, few Democrats would support abortion on demand throughout pregnancy.

***examiner's* note** Although there is overlap, the two main US parties' respective 'platforms' are less important than the candidates elected under each party label.

 ANSWERS

Parties in Congress

Q1 Why do we need to draw a distinction between parties in Congress and those in the various states?

Q2 What proportion of votes in Congress go along party lines?

Q3 How internally divided are congressional parties?

ANSWERS

the main two parties in Congress have few links with the parties operating in individual states

A1 The parties only exist in a meaningful national form once every 4 years (at their national conventions), and within Congress. Congressional parties are, however, rather unlikely coalitions of people who may have little in common beyond their party label.

A2 A party vote is where the majority of one party votes 'yes' and the majority of the other party votes 'no'. In 2008, 53% of House and 52% of Senate votes were party votes.

A3 Republicans from rural areas may have more in common with rural Democrats than with urban Republicans, while urban Democrats may align with Republicans from districts with similar social problems.

examiner's note Conservative Democrat senators, such as Mary Landrieu (Louisiana), are as likely to vote in line with the Republican bloc as with their party.

UK/US party systems, organisation and roles

UK/US comparative

Q1 Identify some arguments against the idea that two-party systems exist in both the USA and the UK.

Q2 How do the organisations of major parties in the UK and the USA differ?

Q3 How much of a role do UK and US parties play in election campaigns?

ANSWERS

both countries are said to have two-party systems, but US parties are far more decentralised

A1 In the same way that the USA can be seen as having '51 party systems' (see Card 80), the UK can be seen as having a series of two party systems (Con/Lab, Lab/LibDem, Con/LibDem) in different parts of the country.

A2 Despite the strengthening of their national organisations since the 1970s, US parties remain largely local institutions. UK parties, in contrast, are highly organised and centralised.

A3 The role of US parties has diminished with the rise of primaries, the mass media and political action committees (PACs). UK parties retain a key role in candidate selection and in campaign finance.

***examiner's* note** The role of UK and US political parties is shaped by how much each political system favours or obstructs their efforts to establish overall control.

 ANSWERS

The end of ideology?

Q1 To what extent were UK and US political parties ever really ideological?

Q2 Give examples that illustrate the way in which UK and US parties have moderated their positions in recent years in order to appeal to a broader range of voters.

ANSWERS

parties' abandonment of old ideologies in favour of becoming effective election-winning machines

A1 US parties have never been truly ideological, although they have taken opposing positions on some key issues (e.g. abortion). UK parties were once said to be ideological, e.g. the Labour Party was formed by the unions and socialist societies to represent the working man.

A2 The Labour and Democratic parties were both forced to moderate their tendency to tax and spend on 'big government' programmes. Blair persuaded the Labour Party to adopt a 'Third Way', dropping Clause 4 and rebranding itself 'New Labour'. Clinton, as a 'new Democrat', announced that the era of big government was over.

***examiner's* note** Some ideological slippage has also taken place in Republican and Conservative camps, e.g. George W. Bush's 'compassionate conservatism' and Cameron's more ready acceptance of those with different sexual orientations.

Minor parties/third-party candidacy

UK/US comparative

Q1 Identify three factors that make life difficult for smaller parties in both the UK and USA.

Q2 What success have smaller parties had in elections?

Q3 Can minor parties be said to succeed in any sense other than breaking through and winning elections?

ANSWERS

A1 Smaller parties struggle to win electoral contests due to the 'winner-takes-all' electoral system. Major party candidates carry a label that voters can identify with and attract better campaign finance.

A2 George Wallace (13%, 46 Electoral College votes in 1968) and Ross Perot (19%, 0 Electoral College votes in 1992) are the best-known third-party presidential candidacies in recent times. The UK Liberal Democrats won 57 seats in the 2010 General Election.

A3 Minor parties can influence the agenda even when they fail in their electoral efforts, e.g. Perot and NAFTA in the USA, and the BNP and immigration in the UK.

***examiner's* note** As well as minor parties, the UK has witnessed the rise of 'single-issue parties' (e.g. the Referendum Party) in recent years.

 89 ANSWERS

Factors affecting pressure group activity

Q1 In what respects does the nature of the USA and the US Constitution favour pressure group activity?

Q2 Why is the USA referred to as a 'pluralist democracy'?

Q3 What are 'access points'?

ANSWERS

the nature of US society, its political culture and the constitutional framework shapes pressure group activity

A1 The range of interests present in US society favours pressure group activity by making it impossible for national parties to perform effective representation. Constitutional fragmentation of power also makes it harder for parties to dominate.

A2 In a pluralist democracy the widest possible range of interests can access and influence the political process. The fragmentation of the US system aids pluralism by making it difficult for an elite to dominate.

A3 Access points are the 'way in' for pressure groups. The many units of government in the US federal system provide numerous access points, as does the initiative process in some states (see Card 64).

***examiner's* note** Some question the portrayal of the USA as a pluralist democracy by pointing to the emergence of enduring elites.

Roles of
US pressure groups

Q1 How important a role do US pressure groups play in representation and participation?

Q2 In what ways are US pressure groups engaged in 'agenda setting'?

Q3 How do pressure groups hold government accountable?

ANSWERS

representation, participation, education, agenda-setting and holding government accountable

A1 As parties struggle to represent the full range of interests present in US society, pressure groups tend to articulate the collective interests of specific groups of individuals.

A2 Pressure groups play a role in setting the political agenda, both directly (by engaging with government) and indirectly (by manipulating the media so as to pressurise politicians).

A3 Pressure groups hold the government accountable through such means as their submissions to congressional committees, their use of legal action and their role in educating the public.

examiner's note Many business groups seek not to hold government to account on behalf of the public but to secure benefits for themselves instead — often at the cost of the public at large (see Card 96).

Classifying US pressure groups

Q1 Are 'interest groups' different from 'pressure groups'?

Q2 Can we apply the UK 'sectional/cause' group model of classification to US pressure groups?

Q3 Does it make any sense to apply the 'insider/outsider' typology to US groups?

Q4 Identify one other typology.

ANSWERS

a range of models has been developed for classifying US pressure groups

A1 No; US commentators often use the term 'interest groups' in the same way that those in the UK would use the term 'pressure groups'.

A2 This model is essentially the same as the 'public/private' interest group typology often referred to in the USA.

A3 Use of this typology is problematic due to fragmentation of power within the federal government and between federal and state governments. Groups can be 'inside' or 'outside' on various different levels.

A4 Anthony Bennett draws a distinction between 'institutional' and 'membership' groups.

examiner's note Although the insider/outsider typology does not fit the US system perfectly, it is possible to identify groups that have had 'insider' status in Washington, e.g. Enron.

Pressure group methods in the USA

Q1 What factors influence a group's choice of methodology?

Q2 What do we mean by 'traditional methods'?

Q3 What is 'lobbying'?

Q4 What kinds of activities might be classed as direct action?

Q5 Give an example of pressure groups using the law to achieve their goals.

ANSWERS

US pressure group methods range from the more traditional to direct and, in some cases, illegal ones

A1 A group's choice of methods will be influenced by factors such as its resources, its status and the nature of its cause.

A2 These include writing to elected representatives, organising marches and petitions, and producing leaflets and posters.

A3 This originally referred to the practice of trying to talk to and influence legislators in lobbies. Many groups now employ professional lobbyists.

A4 Direct action ranges from consumer campaigns and civil disobedience to violence of the type seen against abortion clinics (see Card 97).

A5 The National Association for the Advancement of Colored People's sponsorship of the Brown case in 1954 is a famous example.

***examiner's* note** In the USA and UK, there has been a move towards direct and often violent action in recent years.

 **ANSWERS**

Factors affecting pressure group success

Q1 How important are resources in determining pressure group success?

Q2 To what extent can the nature of a group's cause affect its chances of success?

Q3 What does the term 'group status' mean?

ANSWERS

a pressure group's resources, aims, status and the methods it adopts all determine its success

A1 Successful groups tend to have good human resources. Good financial resources allow them to staff permanent offices and employ lobbyists and lawyers, to sponsor sympathetic candidates and to undermine (through 'attack ads') candidates hostile to the group's cause.

A2 Groups whose ideas are at odds with the views of a significant proportion of the population will struggle to achieve their goals (e.g. pro-life groups). Groups seeking a change involving constitutional amendment are likely to fail (e.g. gun control).

A3 Status is reflected in the extent to which the government is prepared to consult the group. Extreme groups rarely achieve high status.

examiner's note Groups may adopt extreme measures after failing to achieve their aims using traditional methods, e.g. some pro-life groups.

 **ANSWERS**

Political action committees (PACs)

Q1 What led to the emergence of PACs, and how have they increased in number since the 1970s?

Q2 How much money do PACs give to candidates?

Q3 Identify one argument against PACs.

Q4 Examine the link between PAC money and high levels of House and Senate incumbency.

ANSWERS

organisations that collect and channel money to candidates running for political office

A1 PACs proliferated following the 1974 FECA, increasing from around 600 in 1974 to nearly 4,600 in 2010. The Act prevented unions, corporations and trade associations from making campaign contributions directly to candidates. PACs emerged as middlemen.

A2 In 2008 the top 9 PACs gave $25,794,807 to candidates.

A3 PACs give the impression that candidates can be bought by interest groups. Senator Edward Kennedy famously described the legislature as 'the best Congress that money can buy'.

A4 Around 75% of PAC money goes to incumbents. Some argue that PAC money simply follows the candidates who are most likely to win anyway — i.e. incumbents — rather than affecting outcome.

***examiner's* note** The landmark Supreme Court case *Citizens United v. Federal Election Commission* (2010) is likely to have a significant impact on the activities of PACs.

 95 ANSWERS

Special interests in Congress

Q1 What is meant by the term 'iron triangle'?

Q2 Define the terms 'agency capture' and 'revolving door syndrome'.

Q3 How extensive was Enron's network of contacts within Congress?

ANSWERS

the close bonds formed by many pressure groups with legislators and leading bureaucrats

A1 Iron triangle describes the close relationships that can form between a pressure group, the relevant congressional committee and the relevant executive agency or departmental bureau.

A2 Agency capture occurs when an interest group gains control over the agency that should be regulating it. Revolving door syndrome occurs when legislators or senior bureaucrats leave office for well-paid consultancy jobs and former consultants are offered jobs in government.

A3 Enron made contributions to 71 senators and 188 House members. It contacted six of George W. Bush's team prior to its collapse and had awarded five others directorships or consultancies.

***examiner's* note** The actual extent to which special interests can subvert the policy-making and regulatory processes is difficult to gauge.

Abortion and gun control

Q1 Give one reason why pro-life and pro-gun-control groups find it difficult to achieve their respective goals.

Q2 What is the National Rifle Association (NRA)?

Q3 Outline some of the more direct tactics used by pro-life groups since the 1980s.

ANSWERS ⟩⟩

abortion and gun control are both key issues; the former is seen as 'the most divisive issue since slavery'

A1 The right to abortion, established in *Roe v. Wade* (see Card 47), was based on a constitutional 'zone of privacy' identified by the Supreme Court. The 'right to bear arms' is entrenched in the 2nd Amendment. In both areas, therefore, change is unlikely without formal constitutional amendment or significant judicial review.

A2 The NRA campaigns against gun control and is one of the most powerful US pressure groups, with a membership of 4 million.

A3 Picketing of abortion clinics became commonplace in the 1980s. Bomb attacks against clinics and violence against staff increased in the 1990s.

***examiner's* note** The Supreme Court could, in theory, return the right to regulate abortion to states under the 10th Amendment. However, this would entail overturning some enduring legal precedents.

 97 **ANSWERS**

Classification of pressure groups

Q1 Which typology lends itself best to a UK/US comparative analysis of pressure groups?

Q2 Why is the 'insider/outsider' typology less helpful when considering US groups than it is when applied to the UK?

Q3 Illustrate the way in which people might perceive UK and US pressure groups to be working against the public interest.

ANSWERS

the use of pressure group typologies by US and UK commentators to aid analysis

A1 The 'sectional/cause' group typology is one of the most helpful since it equates broadly to the 'public/private' interest group typology often referred to in the USA, and can also be applied to UK groups.

A2 Separation of powers and federal/state divisions mean US pressure groups can be 'inside' or 'outside' on different levels. In the UK, the 'core executive' is key.

A3 Of the Congress that blocked Clinton's regulation of the energy trade, 188 House members and 71 senators had received campaign contributions from Enron. The UK government's planned ban on tobacco advertising in sport did not extend to Formula One motor racing, whose chief had reportedly donated £1,000,000 to the Labour Party.

***examiner's* note** The belief that politicians can be 'bought' can cause political apathy.

(98) ANSWERS

Pressure group methods

UK/US comparative

Q1 Identify the kinds of methods that UK and US pressure groups use.

Q2 Why are US groups more likely to embark on legal action than their UK counterparts?

Q3 How does the issue of abortion demonstrate the differences between UK and US pressure groups?

ANSWERS

the methods adopted by UK and US pressure groups when trying to achieve their aims

A1 UK and US pressure groups still use traditional methods, but they are increasingly turning to direct action as a means of securing more immediate change, e.g. fuel protests in the UK and attacks on abortion clinics in the USA.

A2 The USA is more litigious than the UK, partly due to the entrenchment of positive rights and the power of the higher courts to void inferior actions and regulations. The UK does not have the same 'rights culture' and the courts do not benefit from the same powers of review.

A3 US pro-life groups have adopted a more direct, often violent, approach in recent years than their UK counterparts.

***examiner's* note** In the UK, the Pro-life Alliance has used legal action and electoral candidacy to move the issue of abortion up the agenda.

 **99** **ANSWERS**

Importance of pressure groups

UK/US comparative

Q1 Why might pressure groups be considered more necessary in the USA than in the UK?

Q2 In what respects is the US system of government more accessible to pressure group activity than the UK system?

Q3 Why are some groups more effective than others in both the UK and USA?

ANSWERS

the relative importance of pressure groups in the UK and USA

A1 US pressure groups have the day-to-day role of representing specific interests (see Card 91). This is not as true in the UK, although falling membership of most mainstream parties and spiralling pressure group membership hints at a trend.

A2 The federal system and separation of powers provide numerous 'access points' into the policy-making process. These are not as visible in the UK system due to its unitary nature.

A3 A group's finances are key to its success, as is public receptivity towards its cause. Groups with contacts in and/or access to government may also be more effective.

***examiner's* note** Changes in government and other unforeseen events can see a group's fortunes rise or decline sharply.

 ANSWERS